Warlingham

in old picture postcards

by
Dorothy Tutt

European Library - Zaltbommel/Netherlands MCMLXXXVIII

GB   ISBN 90 288 4634 4 / CIP

© 1988 European Library - Zaltbommel/Netherlands

European Library in Zaltbommel/Netherlands publishes among other things the following series:

IN OLD PICTURE POSTCARDS *is a series of books which sets out to show what a particular place looked like and what life was like in Victorian and Edwardian times. A book about virtually every town in the United Kingdom is to be published in this series. By the end of this year about 300 different volumes will have appeared. 1,500 books have already been published devoted to the Netherlands with the title* **In oude ansichten.** *In Germany, Austria and Switzerland 650, 100 and 25 books have been published as* **In alten Ansichten;** *in France by the name* **En cartes postales anciennes** *and in Belgium as* **In oude prentkaarten** *and/or* **En cartes postales anciennes** *150 respectively 400 volumes have been published.*

For further particulars about published or forthcoming books, apply to your bookseller or direct to the publisher.

INTRODUCTION

The majority of the views in this book are, as the title indicates, of Warlingham, but I have also included a few from Chelsham and Farleigh. Tucked away in a far corner of north-east Surrey, the parishes of Chelsham and Farleigh have remained rural, and indeed Warlingham was also entirely rural up to around a hundred years ago. The main reason for this has been access, or rather the lack of it, though other factors such as land ownership have also played a part. The principal lines of communication, by road and rail, take the easiest way, mainly through the valleys. Only one route, albeit very ancient, comes up onto the plateau, passing through Warlingham and skirting the edge of Chelsham before descending the scarp of the North Downs into the Weald. As a turnpike road it was a failure as very few used it. Today however, in the age of the motor vehicle, it is a busy alternative route to the south.

Warlingham village, approachable only by ascent of a hill which varies in steepness according to the direction from which the approach is made, was not really affected by the opening in 1856 of the branch railway line along the valley from what is now Purley. The construction and eventual opening in 1884 of the second railway line along the valley, which goes through the North Downs to Oxted, combined with the sale of a considerable amount of land over the following years was, however, to generate great change. In the years just before and after the 1884 line opened, a former railway Director, William Gilford, of Redhill, bought much land in Woldingham and purchased the Westhall Farm estate in Warlingham. This land was sold off in large plots for residential building. With the railway available the City business gentleman could now live in the country and work in Town. A quote from the sale notice for the Westhall Farm estate says: 'To keep the Estate select, only *Detached* Houses, to be used as professional or private houses only, of not less value than £500 each, are to be erected on Lots 1 to 38; and of not less value than £400 on Lots 39 to 50, all inclusive; but after the erection of any such Detached House, suitable Lodges, Stabling and Gardeners' Cottages may be erected in connection therewith.' The sale notice describes the area as 'The English Switzerland' no doubt because of the extensive views which some of the houses still enjoy today.

In and near the centre of Warlingham village new villas were built in the period from around 1890 to 1914. These were in pairs or rows, in styles adapted to suit the location. The growth in population affected the available shops, and the first few views capture some of the change taking place around the Green as it lost its rural character. Change came also to the parish church, but the Hamsey Green area beyond, on the Sanderstead side of Warlingham, was not yet affected. The Westhall Farm lands had been attached to the Marden Park estate to the south, but much of Warlingham and Chelsham had been, since the mid-sixteenth century, in the same landownership as Sanderstead. The breaking up and sale of this latter estate started in 1903 and took some years to complete. It was the end of the 1920s before the rash of housebuilding started at Hamsey Green. From Hamsey Green with scenes at Court Farm in peace and war, the route followed by these views crosses over to the Westhall residential area already mentioned. Gas and water works had been established in the valley, and in time both were available in Warlingham. The new houses could be right up to date from the start. In recent years a number of these houses built towards the end of the nineteenth century have been demolished, the site and large garden providing enough space for several detached houses. With a minimal amount of garden these modern houses lack privacy, but it seems this is quite acceptable today.

Beyond Westhall is the School Common, which together with the Green formed the furthest extent of the old open common in this direction. The principal buildings are depicted in the views here. Then after a quick look at the Halliloo valley, which is a borderline area being largely in Woldingham parish, the following views are in Chelsham. The railway has no influence here. Fickleshole, with Fairchilds, is tucked away on the border with Kent, but not nearly so peaceful these days due to the ubiquitous motor car.

The nearby parish is Farleigh, which in 1264 A.D. became part of the endowment of Merton College, Oxford, and remains so today, though subject to local administration. In 1968 this small rural community, whose population has never exceeded one hundred, fought and won the battle to be in Surrey, rather than permanently swallowed up by the London Borough of Croydon. Up to 1955 Farleigh had its own Rector, but then was put with Warlingham and Chelsham, forming a United Benefice.

The view of the Harrow inn brings us back into Warlingham parish, and from here on the views progress back towards the centre of the village, passing the White Lion inn formerly fronted by open common, and so back to the Green. The final views show some of the further changes which had taken place here. These included the building of the Church Hall in 1914. The first Wesleyan Chapel site became a garage, and on the corner of Glebe Road a bank was erected.

I am greatly indebted to Maurice Cooke, John Gent and Roger Packham for two-thirds of these views, the remainder being from my own collection. Space does not permit every corner to be represented, but I hope those included will help new residents, and those of long standing, to obtain added enjoyment from living in this delightful corner of Surrey. The recent publication by the Bourne Society, the local history society, of a book of 'Then and Now' views has proved popular, and is highly recommended to all with an interest in this area of East Surrey. The views of Warlingham it contains are not duplicated in this publication.

The years since 1930 are beyond the scope of this book, but they do now total almost sixty, and the buildings around Warlingham Green have been subject to many further changes during that time. As a resident of over fifty years standing I have seen many of these more recent changes take place, and also the building of many houses in the district. On the credit side the quantity and quality of the open countryside only a step away continues to delight, and its retention, being Green Belt land, is, we trust, secure.

Dorothy Tutt

Warlingham Green.

1. The villas on the left were built in the 1890s but this view of Warlingham Green in 1904 still retains much of the rural character of the village. On the far side, left of the inn sign, stands the first Wesleyan Chapel, built in 1839. A thatched barn is visible just left of the Leather Bottle inn. The sign in the inn yard advertises good stabling available, and conditions underfoot are generally what would be expected in a country village.

Warlingham Green

2. Still in 1904 this view is from alongside the thatched barn which, with another nearby, comprised Mr. Harrup's Livery and Bait Stables. On the further side is Ringer's General Stores, partly obscured by the young trees which were planted on the Green to commemorate Queen Victoria's Jubilee in 1897. The official way around the Green used to be via the Leather Bottle corner, but so much use was made of this short cut past the barn that the Vestry decided in 1889 to make it an official roadway. The present one-way traffic system was first introduced in the later 1940s.

The Old Barn. Warlingham

3. The fine old tree on the corner of the Green by the Leather Bottle, which can be seen in view number 7, lasted for a further sixty years but not so the barn. In August 1905 barn and stables were demolished, and the greater part burnt on site. Such an exciting bonfire naturally attracted the children. In the background is Yew Tree Cottage, some part of which still stands today but obscured by modern building on what was formerly the front garden.

4. The barn was demolished because in July 1905 the land had been sold by Richard Ramsey Bond, the younger, to a Caterham builder, C.E. Kenworthy. Bradford Buildings, dated 1905, was soon erected, a block of four modern shops with living accommodation, and a yard with stabling behind. This view was taken in 1907. A bank now has the corner position and the adjoining premises. The other two shops have also been converted into one.

5. This closer view of Ringer's Stores, which included the village Post Office, is dated 1908. The Union of London and Smiths Bank Ltd, now occupies the extreme left of the block. The low building behind the fence is the premises of J. Hipgrave, photographer, whose varied work included some local view postcards.

Old Cottages, Croydon Road, Warlingham.

6. The creation of the roadway, seen in view number 2, made the Green triangular in shape. This view, dated 1908, shows the front of the villas opposite the Leather Bottle inn, and beyond them an old cottage. John Hassell's watercolour of 1820s date shows a cottage here. The main fabric was eighteenth century or earlier, the dormer windows being a nineteenth century addition. The building was demolished in 1957, and a block of shops erected on the site.

1777 Warlingham Green.

7. This view of 1904 shows the small shops on the Leather Bottle side of the Green. As yet one block still remains as cottages with small front gardens. To the left is Ringer's other shop. The Leather Bottle inn dates in part from the eighteenth century. On the far right is Mill House. The windmill, destroyed by fire in 1865, had stood some way back in the field behind. In the early 1950s Mill House was demolished, and Shelton Avenue was extended, creating a circular estate. The development included a permanent building for Warlingham Library, and this was officially opened on 1st May 1954.

Ringer & Sons, Warlingham.

The Village Green, Warlingham.

2405.

8. A general view, dated about 1912, shows the Green as rough, criss-crossed with the paths worn by day after day use. On the right, outside Ringer's shop, there is a cobbled gutter, and the footpath is raised up slightly above the road level.

All Saints. — Upper Warlingham.

C. J. Sluiter, Whyteleafe.

9. Leaving Warlingham Green by the road to Sanderstead a footpath set diagonally across the field on the right led to All Saints' Church. There was a 'kissing' gate and a field gate at both ends of the path. The larger gate was necessary to give access for funerals, or for movement of the animals kept in the field. This view is dated 1904. In 1907 Church Road was made on much the same line as the old footpath.

10. The population of Warlingham was increasing, and by the early 1890s the need arose to enlarge the church. This view of All Saints' before the enlargement of 1893 shows that it was a simple building of mid-thirteenth century date, Early English in style. The internal measurements were 57 by 19 feet. Several interesting features were uncovered as the work progressed, one of the most important being that the original level of the chancel floor was seven inches lower than the nave floor.

ALL SAINTS, WARLINGHAM.

11. Enlarging All Saints' Church involved destroying the west wall and the greater part of the south nave wall. Some of the graveyard had to be cleared. The nave was extended 27 feet to the west, and a new bell turret was constructed. The two-light window, to the right of the porch in view number 10, is, from this angle, hidden by the eastern end of the roof of the new south aisle.

All Saints Church, Warlingham.

12. This interior view to the east dates from the later 1920s. The east window is of mid-fourteenth century date, replacing earlier lancets. The north wall of the chancel is 30 inches thick. The old structure ended just west of the lancet window on the left of this view, and the join of old and new work is visible in the plasterwork.

Interior All Saints Church, Warlingham.

13. This view to the west, also dating from the later 1920s, shows the gallery erected to take the organ. There had been a gallery in the earlier nineteenth century to accommodate the live musicians who supported the singing, but it was removed in 1867. This gallery remained until 1957. Electric light was installed in 1934.

14. All Saints' churchyard was enlarged in September 1901, June 1916, and again in June 1927. These views date from the latter occasion when land was given by Mr. E.H. Hodgkinson in memory of his father, Sir George Edmund Hodgkinson. Here the procession is just moving off. The churchwardens, Mr. C.L. Lockton J.P. (on the left) and Mr. A.C. Jones, are followed by the Bishop of Woolwich.

15. The procession was led by the cross bearer and two choir members. Behind the choir and clergy came the Warlingham Band, the Parochial Church Council, and members of the congregation. During the walk around the two acre extension the band accompanied the singing of psalms and hymns. It was not a very warm afternoon, and several people carried an umbrella.

"Warlingham." Sy.
All Saints' Church. June 6th 1927.
Consecration of New Burial Ground.

16. The Service of Consecration of the extension to the churchyard included the reading out of the legal document of the gift of the land. This was done by the Vicar, Reverend F.R. Dickinson. The Bishop of Woolwich gave an address, and the service ended with prayers.

17. Hamsey Green Pond was by far the largest in the district, and this view taken in 1914 shows about two-thirds of it. At the time of the 1866 Inclosure it was said to be some 1600 square yards. Change came after the land around was sold in the 1920s, and today it is very small indeed.

HAMSEY GREEN POND, Warlingham Surrey.

18. It was around 1850 when Walter Bex started his business near the pond at Hamsey Green. The trades he followed were those of builder, decorator, shopfitter, cabinetmaker, wheelwright and undertaker. This scene of 1910 shows that the ladies of the household were, at this time, also busy. Many tea gardens existed at this period. Here there were three and a half acres of grounds, and probably simple entertainment such as swings. The house still stands, tucked away behind the petrol station.

19. Warlingham Court Farm was situated near to the parish boundary with Sanderstead. The approach from Tithepit Shaw Lane remains, also the cottages set alongside it, but the house was demolished in 1967. This view of around 1910 shows the farm entrance and some of the extensive farm buildings.

Court Farm House, Upper Warlingham

20. This closer view of Court Farm house was, like the previous view, published by J.H. Hinton. The Hintons lived at Court Farm, and this card, sent by Mr. Hinton in 1909, confirms a booking for a church outing. Here was yet another place providing refreshments and entertainments, very popular for Sunday School outings. Built on an earlier site, much of this house dated back to the eighteenth century. It had a very large kitchen, and extensive cellars.

J.H. Winton,
Warlingham.

Up the Steps to Court Farm, Warlingham.   2395

21. A visitor to Court Farm Pleasure Grounds was able to follow a well-defined route up from Whyte-leafe, in part set out with steps as this view of 1910 shows.

22. A group of ladies pause for a moment on the final flight of rustic steps up to Court Farm, 1905.

Orchard with View of House and Refreshment Pavillions.   Court Farm Upper Warlingham

23. A view, also of 1905, showing something of the rear of Court Farm and the area set aside for amusements and refreshments. Swings are over on the right.

3146. C. Company, Empire Batt? Royal Fusiliers. H. Hodgson Whyteleafe.

24. On 12th September 1914 the newly formed 17th (Empire Battalion) Royal Fusiliers arrived at Upper Warlingham Station and proceeded up the hill to Court Farm, led by the local band. Initially they were divided into A, B, C and D Companies. This scene and those that follow were recorded during the early weeks of the camp.

B. Company Pay Day.
Empire Batt. Royal Fusiliers.
3145.
H. Hodgson.
Whyteleafe.

25. The camp had a miserable start. Tents had been erected on ground covered with thick long grass, and a thunderstorm which broke overhead drenched everything. The men had no groundsheets or blankets, but the local people soon came to their aid. Indeed, throughout the time the Battalion was in Warlingham the local residents were most generous and hospitable towards these volunteers. December 1914 was the wettest for sixty years – over 10 inches of rain was recorded in Warlingham. Huts eventually replaced the tents, and some men were billeted in the village – one hopes before the 12 inches of snow that fell on 22nd January 1915! That spring there was a Bourne flow.

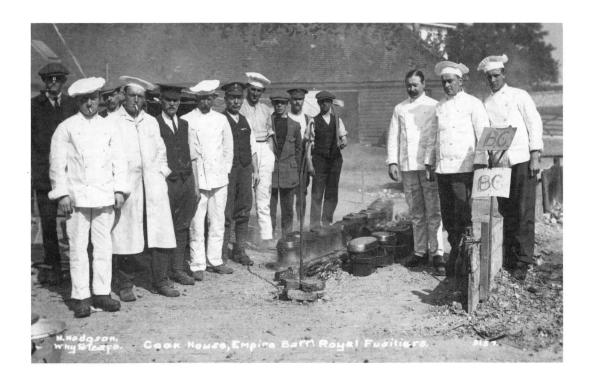

26. Men from the National Reserve Battalion were soon brought in, all old soldiers and many qualified as instructors and cooks. Order emerged from chaos, and life in the camp included plenty of sport and amusements as well as the hard training. The senior officers were frequently entertained by the Hintons at the farmhouse.

Court Farm Camp, Empire Batt, Royal Fusiliers.

27. Local people chat with the men in the shade of the well-known maple trees. Initially they had no uniform or equipment. They used wooden substitutes for rifles, but in November 1914 a few did arrive – one to every six men. By the end of the year they had all been issued with blue uniforms and forage caps. This was the peacetime fatigue dress, and greatly disliked. In June 1915 the Battalion moved on to Nottinghamshire, all now in khaki and having received basic training.

General View, Whyteleafe, from Court Farm Camp.

28. In the centre of this view, taken in 1914, is Lower Barn Farm, perhaps better remembered as King's Farm, which stood at the junction of Tithepit Shaw Lane with Workhouse Lane. Now called Hillbury Road, Workhouse Lane was the old and only direct route from Warlingham village to the valley until Westhall Road was made. The Workhouse Cottages were on the level land at the top of the hill, and ceased to be used as such in 1834. This view shows how splendid this valley was before the eruption of houses.

Warlingham Hill. Surrey. 2

29. The branch railway line along the valley was opened in 1856, and a couple of years later part of Workhouse Lane was widened slightly. The bends on the steep upper stretch remained unaltered until recent years, when the road was opened right out. The change of name to Hillbury Road was introduced in the early 1900s, but some years passed before the old name was completely forgotten. This view taken in the 1920s shows the sturdy flint wall, a small part of which still remains. Searchwood Road goes off to the right at this point.

Warlingham. West Hall from the Golf Links.

30. This view, dated 1905, was taken from across the valley. A number of the houses built on this side of the Westhall estate are visible, also the railway cutting and Succombs Hill. The large property on the right is Dorincourt, now replaced by an even larger block of flats. Growth of trees over the years obscured the houses from view, but many have now reappeared following the devastation caused by the storm of hurricane force on 16th October 1987.

West Hall Warlingham

C. J. Sluiter, Whyteleafe.

31. This view is dated about 1906. These are the first houses built on the lower stretch of Westhall Road, and the four furthest from this viewpoint are on the skyline of view number 32. This land was, until sold in the early 1900s, part of the Sanderstead estate held by the Arkwrights. A section of the old footpath from the valley away down on the left still exists. From the extreme right of this view it passes between the gardens to emerge in Searchwood Road which continues the route of the old path to the junction with Hillbury Road.

32. Opposite the houses built on the lower stretch of Westhall Road the ground falls away sharply. This scene shows a motor accident which occurred in October 1906. There is every indication that the car, registration number A6890, came down from the road high above, finishing up in what was in 1906 a working quarry! Houses now fill every usable piece of ground, including the quarry.

33. When the railway was constructed access was provided for the established routes which would otherwise have been severed. One of these was from by Well Farm, where an archway was made. The path is clearly marked on the 1869 O.S. map going straight up the hillside to Westhall Wood. When houses were built on the hillside the path was made easier by the formation of these flights of steps, seen here in about 1920. Caterham also has a Jacob's Ladder.

Eden College, Warlingham, Surrey

34. This house, to one side of Jacob's Ladder, was a school for young ladies for many years. This view dates from around 1905. In the 1930s it was known as 'Ravenscroft' the name of the house, and took day girls and boarders. A former pupil, who was a boarder, has said it was a very strict establishment. Over fifteen years have passed since this house was demolished.

West Hall, Warlingham.

35. This view, dating from 1909, is of the corner where Landscape Road, coming from the right, joins Westhall Road. The footpath, named Jacob's Ladder, also comes out at this junction.

36. This view, dated 1905, shows the stretch of new road made on the line of the old footpath, part of which remains as Jacob's Ladder. On the left is The Laurels, one of the first houses built in the development of Westhall. At this point the Parish Road, now called Narrow Lane, connects Westhall with Succombs Hill and the valley.

West Hall, Warlingham.

5092.

Ringer & Son.
Warlingham.

37. This view, dated about 1912, shows how narrow Westhall Lane was as it passed Westhall farm. The house in the distance is The Laurels. It was demolished in 1985, and three modern houses now occupy the corner plot.

The Schools, Warlingham.

Ringer & Son's
Warlingham.

38. At the time of the 1866 Inclosure two pieces of the common land were set aside for the use of the local people. The smaller became the Green, and the other, an expanse of over four acres, was named the Common Recreation Ground. It became generally known as 'School Common' after the school and schoolhouse, seen in this view of 1911, were built on the corner nearest to Westhall. The school opened in December 1874 with 75 pupils, and closed in July 1982 with 36. The buildings stood empty for over five years but now alterations and additions are turning them into residential property.

39. For over 300 years this building, shown here in a photograph dated 1925, was Warlingham Vicar-age. It is situated facing the common, and a glebe field lies adjacent to it. Various structural changes have been made over the years, particularly to the front façade. It passed into private hands in 1984, and the Vicarage is now a house in Chapel Road, of early 1900s date.

40. Reverend G.R. Macaulay M.A. came to Warlingham as Curate in April 1896. Four years later, when the Vicar moved on to Wotton, Oxfordshire, he was instituted as Vicar of Warlingham with the Chapelry of Chelsham annexed. He married Dorothy, daughter of the churchwarden, Charles L. Lockton, and remained as Vicar until April 1925. That same year an anonymous benefactor purchased the gift of the living, which up to that time had belonged to the Lord of the Manor, and handed it over to the Bishop of Southwark.

School Common, Warlingham.

Quittenton's Photo Series.

41. Like the Green the School Common is triangular in shape. This view, dated 1910, is of the corner nearest to the Green, with Leas Road off to the left and Westhall Road to the right. The cottages on the right were demolished in 1959. Boots were the usual footwear for the children at this period, and even the smallest schoolchild wore a hat.

Warlingham. The Alms Houses.

42. This view, taken from the common in 1904, shows the almshouses, which stand at the junction of Chapel Road with Leas Road. They were built in 1675 by Harman Atwood, Lord of the Manor. There are four small houses, two for Warlingham people, one for Chelsham and one for Sanderstead. The central house was originally intended for the use of a curate of the parish. A small school was started here, and to provide more space a one room extension was built at the rear. This addition, now known as the Mission Room, was rebuilt in 1857, and remained the village school until 1874.

Near Fir Tree Wood
UPPER WARLINGHAM.

43. This view of around 1910 shows the further end of Leas Road, sometimes called Bug Hill Road, as it curves round to the top of Bug Hill. Most of Fir Tree Wood was cut down when Beechwood Lane was laid out.

The Leas. Warlingham. 2

44. This view of the Leas was taken in the early 1920s. Some of the buildings of Halliloo farm are visible on the far right. Over the years the growth of trees has enhanced the beauty of this valley, but the hurricane of 16th October 1987 took its toll here also.

Near Worms Heath.
Surrey.

45. At the head of the Halliloo valley, on the road from Warlingham to Worms Heath, is Slynes Pond and Slynes Green. The pond remains, but due to the widening of the road, and also the growth of trees and bushes, Slynes Green has virtually disappeared. This view is dated 1910.

The Beeches, Warlingham

46. The avenue of beech trees at Botley Hill is pictured here from a postcard of about 1914. Many people still remember with affection these fine trees whose branches met overhead, making a leafy tunnel. Regrettably, because several were found to be decayed, all were cut down, and so for the past twenty years or so Botley Hill farm has been exposed to all weathers. The very popular tearooms at this farm were open for 51 years, from 1936 to 1987.

Road to Worms Heath, Warlingham.

47. Returning towards Warlingham, past Worms Heath and Slynes Green, this stretch of road, apart from being widened, looks much the same today as it did in this view of 1908.

Chelsham Green.

C. J. Sluiter, Whyteleafe.

48. In 1904, when this scene was photographed, the grazing cattle would be unlikely to be disturbed by more than the occasional horse and cart. This stretch of grass, across the road from the Hare and Hounds public house, still exists today. The road, however, is very seldom free of traffic. The trees in the distance are those in view number 47.

Chelsham Common PP4

49. The original Bull inn was on Bull common, which is away to the right of this view of Chelsham common, taken in 1910. The above building dates from the later nineteenth century. All the buildings to the right of the inn have been demolished, and a bungalow has replaced the cottages on the left. Also on the left, visible above the trees, is the clock tower of Warlingham Park Hospital.

50. The land for Croydon Mental Hospital was purchased in 1898. The foundation stone was laid in 1900, and the official opening ceremony was held in June 1903. It stands beyond Chelsham common, the tall clock tower being visible from a considerable distance away. The name was changed to Warlingham Park Hospital in 1937. This photograph was taken in the 1920s.

1778 Chelsham Church.

51. St. Leonard's Church, Chelsham, photographed in 1904. The oldest part of the fabric dates from the thirteenth century. Considerable restoration work was carried out in the nineteenth century. There has been no need to enlarge this church, as in this rural area far from the railway the population is small. In medieval times Chelsham would seem to have been of more importance than Warlingham. The railed tomb beneath the overhanging yew tree is that of Alderman Thomas Kelly, Lord Mayor of London in 1836, who lived in Chelsham as a child.

52. Fickleshole Cottages, of late seventeenth century date, as they were in 1910. The pair on the left were demolished some years ago. The White Bear, a very popular public house, was originally only in the far end house but now extends throughout the block. Beyond the low wall on the left is the pond belonging to Fickleshole farm. It is known that a pond existed in the vicinity, possibly in this same spot, as long ago as the fourteenth century.

THE WHITE BEAR INN CHELSHAM.

53. This postcard shows the White Bear inn as it was in the 1920s. The variety of window is interesting here. That above the bear's head is of the horizontal sliding type, a few of which still remain in old cottages. It is said that the bear was brought out here from London, a prank on the part of the young gentry of the time.

Farleigh Church

54. This is a little Norman church, dating from about 1080 A.D., in a very rural area. It is dedicated to St. Mary the Virgin, and this postcard, dated 1905, shows it from the south-west viewpoint. The walls are extremely thick, 36 inches in the nave and 32 inches in the chancel. The vestry was added in the nineteenth century. The porch seen here covering the west door was expertly rebuilt in 1911, using old oak. In 1264 A.D. Farleigh became part of the endowment of Merton College, Oxford, and remains so to this day.

Farleigh Court.

Scattergood's
Photo Series.

55. The original house is thought to have been built in the eleventh century as was the church nearby. It was a moated site and some traces still remain. The present building dates from the seventeenth century. Since 1912, the date of this view, the ground floor windows on this façade have been enlarged, and the door altered. It is an active farm, the farmer being a tenant of Merton College, Oxford.

A Happy New Year To you All

Farleigh Common.

Scattergood's Photo Series.

56. This particular stretch of common does, in fact, have the name Great Farleigh Green. Little Farleigh Green is right over on the further side of the parish beyond the church and Farleigh Court Farm. This view dates from 1912. The roof of Thatched Cottage, which dates from the sixteenth and seventeenth centuries, is just visible amongst the trees to the left of the car. The road is still narrow today, and is used a great deal by traffic travelling between Selsdon and Warlingham.

Elm Farm, Farleigh Common.

57. Elm Farm is shown here on a postcard dated 1911. The building dates from the seventeenth century and still stands back from the road, there being a good width of common at this point. In 1907 Isabel, former companion to Dorothy Lockton (who married the Vicar of Warlingham), married Charles Alfred Scott and came to live at Elm Farm. Many people had their milk from Elm Farm Dairy, and Charles Scott spent much of his day travelling around the district in his two-wheeled cart pulled by a patient horse named Dinah.

THE HARROW INN.

58. Returning across the parish boundary from Farleigh into Warlingham the first building on the right is the Harrow inn. It stands, as does the Leather Bottle, at the extreme corner of the former common land. In the seventeenth century the building was called Aynescombes, and later on it became an ale house. This view is dated 1908. Until the building of the mental hospital there were very few houses in this furthest corner of Warlingham.

Chelsham Parsonage.

59. Chelsham Parsonage was on Harrow common, the nearest building being the Harrow inn. This photograph, taken around 1920, also shows the rear of houses in Farleigh Road. Part of the Parsonage was occupied by the school, which had been started in the 1830s by the then curate, Reverend Richard Fell. In 1905 the school moved to new premises near Chelsham common, and in 1955 a new Parsonage was built by St. Christopher's Church in Chelsham Road. Subsequently the old house and its large enclosure of land was sold, and it now stands in Parsonage Close.

The Forge, Warlingham.

60. Farleigh Road was formerly a track following the edge of the open common. On this road, and not far from the centre of Warlingham, was the blacksmith's forge. The Blanchard family lived and worked here for many years. The sign says 'Smith, Farrier, Coachbuilder and Wheelwright', and the view is dated 1910. Only the cottages remain, and they are now one house called Forge Cottage. A modern house stands on the site of the forge, and the house in the background, 'The Meadows', was demolished in 1987. There is now a small close of detached houses on this site.

61. This house is Box Cottage, as it was about 1908. It stood just around the corner from the forge, at the point where Bond Road meets Farleigh Road. It is better remembered as Webb's Cottage, from the family who lived there for many years. In 1890 Richard Ramsey Bond, the elder, bought this house, and nearby land of over four acres in extent, for £600. Boxwood Way now covers most of the land, and a modern bungalow has replaced Box Cottage.

62. An unusual view, of about 1912, showing the side and rear of the buildings in views number 60 and 61. Only the Forge Cottage and Paddock Cottage, which carries the date 1859, remain today.

63. This view, dated 1903, shows the ancient cottages which stood near the Horseshoe public house on the corner where Mint Walk meets Farleigh Road. Local materials, flint and bricks, are used here. When they were demolished in the late 1930s one house was found to have an old tombstone as a doorstep.

Warlingham "The Horse Shoe."

64. A view of 1908 showing the Horseshoe public house and the cottages nearby, pictured on number 63. There used to be a large pond in the foreground, on the edge of the open common. These buildings were demolished in the late 1930s, and the new Horseshoe was built set back from the road.

65. The White Lion inn dates in part from the seventeenth century and, not surprisingly, the older part is set very low in relation to the modern road level. The row of trees in this view of 1904 helped to protect the building as well as adding greatly to the scene. Sadly the last one had to be removed in 1979.

Warlingham—Meet of the Hounds

A. J. Braid, Caterham Valley

66. Warlingham was occasionally enlivened by the arrival of the Old Surrey and Burstow Hunt. This scene outside the White Lion is dated 1904.

Wesleyan Chapel & Village Hall, Warlingham.

Quittenton's Photo Series.

67. On the left of this view of 1910 is the Working Man's Club, opened in November 1902. Baths were available here, a luxury not found in the ordinary cottage. Main drainage did not come to Warlingham until 1929. Across the road stands the second Wesleyan Chapel, built in 1871 and enlarged in 1908. It was demolished in 1960, when a third building was erected further along the road. The Turkey Oak still stands outside what is now called the Village Hall.

68. This is a scene taken alongside the Working Man's Club, the occasion being the Church Parade on 26th August 1923. From time to time funds were raised to help the Cottage Hospital in Caterham. This hospital, which opened in 1902, existed until the mid-1980s, the building being finally demolished early in 1987. The side of the old Horseshoe public house is visible on the left of this picture.

69. A general view of about 1913 shows that there is little traffic to worry the people or the dogs who wander all over the road. On the right, partly obscured by a tree, is Aberdeen House. Built as a butcher's shop it has remained so to this day.

Soldiers Club. Upper Warlingham.

70. From 1912 onwards fund raising events were held to collect money for the building of a Church Hall. It was built in 1914, then in 1915 commandeered and used for a few months as hospital accommodation. From 1916 to 1919 it was used as a soldiers' club. It was 1922 before the outstanding debt for the construction of the hall was finally extinguished.

Soldiers Club,
Warlingham

71. The Church Hall was used as a soldiers' club from 16th October 1916 to 1st April 1919. Men often came over to Warlingham from the camp at Woldingham as that village had no public house and they found the company agreeable. They were at the Woldingham camp to rest and recover from war wounds, it being a convalescent home by this time.

The Green, Warlingham"

Photo by G. Read.

72. The War Memorial was the work of Mr. J.E. Taylerson, and has the title 'Shielding the Defence-less'. It was unveiled and dedicated at a Service on 4th December 1921. This view was taken shortly afterwards. The gas street lamps are still few in number.

THE GREEN
WARLINGHAM. 42.

73. This view of the Green, dating from the later 1920s, shows the German Howitzer presented to Warlingham in 1920 by the 17th Battalion Royal Fusiliers. The paths were laid out in the spring of 1923, and the stone seat given to complete the scene. The gun was removed for salvage in the Second World War, but the plaque from it is preserved in the East Surrey Museum.

74. Small 'Dame' schools still flourished in the 1920s and 1930s. One of these was held in one of the pair of houses facing the Green called Blenheim Villas. Mrs. G. Reed was the teacher at Blenheim House school, and this photograph, taken in the garden at the rear, shows her with her pupils in 1928.

The Green, Upper Warlingham   6

75. This view, dating from the 1920s, provides a closer look at the Leather Bottle inn and the shops beyond. The stone, almost certainly a waymarker, still rests at the foot of the inn sign, but is now embedded in the road island. The lamp attached to the post has a decorative bracket.

76. Another view from the 1920s shows that winter can be very severe on occasion. On 26th December 1927 snow started to fall, and soon drifts twelve feet deep blocked the roads, cutting Warlingham off for ten days. The snowfall of January 1987 is also likely to be remembered, it being so heavy roads were blocked and the railway was put out of action for some hours.